Saturn

Tim Goss

Heinemann Library
Chicago, Illinois

© 2003 Reed Educational & Professional Publishing
Published by Heinemann Library,
an imprint of Reed Educational & Professional Publishing,
Chicago, Illinois

Customer Service 888-454-2279

Visit our website at www.heinemannlibrary.com

Layout by Roslyn Broder
Illustrations by Calvin J. Hamilton
Printed in China

07 06
10 9 8 7 6 5 4 3

Library of Congress Cataloging-in-Publication Data
Goss, Tim, 1958-
 Saturn / by Tim Goss.
  v. cm. -- (The universe)
Includes bibliographical references and index.
Contents: Where in the sky is Saturn? -- How's the weather on Saturn? -- How did Saturn get its rings? -- What's special about Saturn? -- What would I see if I went to Saturn? -- What is inside Saturn? -- Could I ever go to Saturn?
 ISBN 1-58810-915-1 (HC) , 1-4034-0616-2 (Pbk)
 1. Saturn (Planet)--Juvenile literature. [1. Saturn (Planet)] I. Title. II. Series.
 QB671 .G67 2002
 523.46--dc21
                         2002000811

Acknowledgments
The author and publisher are grateful to the following for permission to reproduce copyright material: p. 4 NASA/Ames Research Center; pp. 5T, 24 NASA/Ames Research Center/Rick Guidice; p. 5B Vince Streano/Corbis; p. 6 D. Van Ravenswaay/Photo Researchers, Inc.; pp. 7, 8, 11, 12, 14, 16, 17, 18, 19, 20B, 21, 25, 26, 28, 29 NASA/JPL/Caltech; p. 9 Phil Nicholson/Cornell University, Steve Larson/University of Arizona, and NASA; p. 10 Erich Karkoschka/University of Arizona Lunar & Planetary Lab and NASA; p. 13 Reta Beebe/New Mexico State University, D. Gilmore and L. Bergeron/Space Telescope Science Institute, and NASA; p. 15 NASA/JPL/Caltech/National Space Science Data Center; p. 20T NASA/U.S. Geological Survey; pp. 22, 23 Courtesy of Calvin J. Hamilton/www.solarviews.com

Cover photograph by NASA/JPL/Caltech

The publisher would like to thank Geza Gyuk and Diana Challis of the Adler Planetarium for their comments in the preparation of this book.

Some words are shown in bold, **like this.** You can find out what they mean by looking in the glossary.

Contents

Where in the Sky Is Saturn? 4

How Did Saturn Get Its Rings? 7

What's Special About Saturn?. 9

How's the Weather on Saturn?. 11

What Would I See if I Went to Saturn? 14

What Is Inside Saturn? 22

Could I Ever Go to Saturn? 23

Fact File. 28

Glossary. 30

More Books to Read 31

Index 32

Where in the Sky Is Saturn?

On a clear night, when the **stars** are shining brightly, you might see one star that does not shine or twinkle. If you do, you are not looking at a star. You may be looking at the **planet** Saturn. With a **telescope,** you can see the rings around Saturn and even some of the planet's **moons.**

This image shows the true color of Saturn. It is a combination of two pictures of the planet.

Saturn is the sixth planet from the **Sun** in our **solar system.** Saturn is the second largest planet. Only Jupiter is larger than Saturn. If Saturn were hollow, you could fit 760 Earths inside of it.

The solar system

The solar system is made of all the planets, **comets,** and **asteroids** that circle the Sun. The Sun's **gravity** pulls on all of the objects in our solar system. If it were not for the pull of the Sun, the planets would travel in straight lines. This would send them out into deep space! The force of gravity keeps the planets in regular paths around the Sun called **orbits.**

Who found Saturn?

People have been looking at Saturn for a long time, possibly since prehistoric times. They were able to do so because you can see the planet without a telescope. They did not know for sure what they were looking at, though. In 1610, the famous Italian **astronomer** Galileo Galilei (1564–1642) used an early telescope and saw the planet more closely. He noticed the rings, but the image was fuzzy and the rings looked like "handles" on the planet or perhaps moons next to it. Dutch scientist Christiaan Huygens (1629–1693) used a better telescope in 1655 and figured out a few years later that the "handles" around Saturn were actually rings.

Saturn is the sixth planet from the Sun.

How did Saturn get its name?

The name Saturn comes from the Latin name *Saturnus.* Saturnus was the Roman god of seeds, planting, and farming. People usually honored him at harvest festivals. In Rome, the capital of Italy, you can still see what is left of the temple built to honor Saturnus.

How does Saturn move through space?

Saturn is the sixth **planet** from the **Sun.** It is ten times farther from the Sun than Earth, so Saturn has to travel a much longer path to loop once around the Sun. This loop around the Sun is called a planet's **orbit.** The time if takes for a planet to make one orbit is called a **year.** Earth's year is 365 **days** long. Saturn's year is 29.5 times as long as an Earth year. This is because Saturn has farther to go and moves more slowly than Earth.

Saturn moves more slowly than Earth in its orbit, because the force of the Sun's gravity is weaker so far out.

We have day and night on Earth because Earth spins as it **revolves** around the Sun. Sometimes we are facing the Sun and it is day. When it is night, the part of the Earth we live on is facing away from the Sun. An Earth day is 24 hours long. Saturn spins much faster than Earth. A day on Saturn lasts only about 10.5 hours.

How Did Saturn Get Its Rings?

Scientists are not sure where the chunks in Saturn's rings came from. They may have formed after Saturn became a planet. They might be small pieces from ancient **moons** that were broken when **comets** or **meteorites** crashed into them.

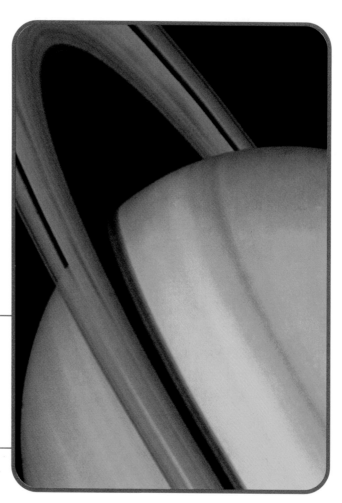

Saturn has four main ring groups and three more faint, narrow groups with gaps in between them.

Cassini's Gap

In 1675, the French **astronomer** Giovanni Cassini found a dark area in Saturn's "ring." He later discovered that the dark area was really a hole or a gap. This meant that Saturn had at least two separate rings. Cassini's Gap is there because ring particles that orbit at that distance from the planet get thrown out of orbit. This happens because the particles in that section are repeatedly pulled on by the moons of Saturn. Today we know that the gap is not empty. It contains at least 100 smaller rings called **ringlets.**

What are the rings made of?

Before there were powerful **telescopes** and **space probes,** people thought that Saturn had one ring. They thought the ring was a single, solid object. As early as 1660, a scientist named Jean Chapelain suggested that the rings were made of many small objects. Since almost everyone was convinced that the ring was solid, they ignored Chapelain. Almost 200 years passed before James Clerk Maxwell's (1831–1879) studies showed that the rings were made of more particles than anyone could count.

Today we know that Saturn's rings are made of frozen water, dust, and maybe some bits of rock. Pieces of ice in Saturn's rings can be smaller than your hand or as long as a school bus. The chunks form a ring when they travel close together in **orbits** around Saturn. The rings reflect a lot of light because they are made mostly of ice.

The different colors in this image represent possible differences in the chemicals found in the rings of Saturn.

What's Special About Saturn?

It could float in water

Even though Saturn is so huge, if you could put it in an ocean, Saturn would float. That is because Saturn has the lowest **density** of all the **planets.** Density is a comparison of how much stuff an object is made of to how much space it takes up. A ball of cotton is less dense than a rock of the same size. Earth is much smaller than Saturn, but it has a much greater density.

Sometimes the rings disappear

In 1612, two years after Galileo first saw the rings of Saturn, he looked again and saw that the "handles" had disappeared. In later observations, he saw the rings again. Dutch scientist Huygen studied Saturn's rings and predicted that in the summer of 1671 they would "disappear." He was right. Where did the rings go?

This image of Saturn was taken at sunset. The rings appear as just a thin line across the center of the planet, but show more detail at the sides.

Traveling on a tilt

Saturn moves through space on a tilted **axis,** just like Earth does. This means that scientists usually see the rings at an angle. They see part of the top or the bottom of the rings. Huygen discovered that every fourteen or fifteen years, Earth passes through the plane of Saturn's rings. This means that the tilts of the two **planets** are lined up so scientists on Earth see only the edge of the rings. It is called a **ring-plane crossing.**

The rings are from 33 feet (10 meters) to 328 feet (100 meters) thick. Across a distance of millions of miles of space, it is hard to see something that narrow, even with a **telescope.** The glare from the rings almost disappears with an edge-on view. So, it looks like the rings are not there.

Without the rings reflecting sunlight, it is easier to see the **moons.** *In this edge-on view of Saturn, you can see six of the planet's moons and the shadow of another.*

How's the Weather on Saturn?

If you ever plan a trip to Saturn, you had better have a very warm space suit. Temperatures in Saturn's **atmosphere** can get as low as −285°F (−176°C). That is more than twice as cold as the coldest temperatures on Earth.

Strong winds on Saturn push the cloud layers around the planet at very high speeds. **Space probes** have measured wind on Saturn moving at speeds faster than 1,100 miles per hour (1,770 kilometers per hour). This is about four times as fast as the quickest race cars on Earth.

Every day's weather report: windy and cloudy

The winds blow every **day** on Saturn. The planet is always covered with clouds. Earth's clouds usually look white because they contain mostly water droplets and ice crystals made of water. Saturn's clouds appear yellow, red, and brown. The yellow comes from the ammonia crystals that cause the clouds to form. When other elements, such as phosphorus, also get into Saturn's clouds, they cause other colors to appear.

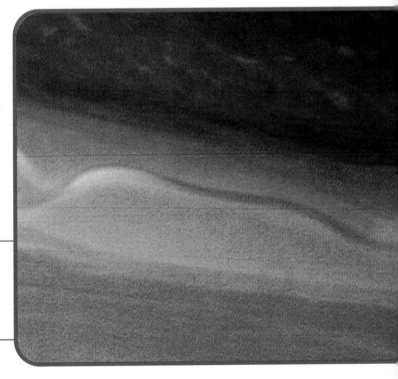

In this image of Saturn's atmosphere, a wave in the clouds is visible.

Do you like stormy weather?

About every 30 Earth **years,** there is a huge storm on Saturn that lasts about a month. This storm is called the Great White Spot. The clouds in this storm are very bright. You can see them with a **telescope** from your own backyard. As the storm comes to an end, the spot stretches out into a white stripe across the **planet.**

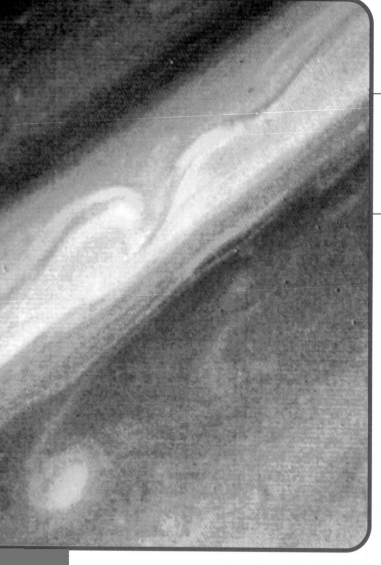

Winds have made the "6"-shaped pattern you see in the lower left corner of this image.

There are other storms that happen on Saturn, too. Some of them cover an area as large as the diameter of Earth. During storms on Saturn, lightning often flashes from cloud to cloud.

*The white feature just above the rings, near the planet's **equator**, is a storm.*

Why is Saturn so cold?

Saturn only receives about one percent of the amount of sunlight that Earth does. This is because Saturn is almost ten times farther away from the **Sun.** This can only warm the planet a little bit. In fact, Saturn gives off about twice as much heat as it receives from the Sun. The heat given off by the planet mostly comes from its **core.**

When Saturn first formed, much of the planet's heat was trapped in its **atmosphere** and core. Saturn has slowly been losing that heat ever since. Today the temperature of Saturn's outer layer is about –274°F (–170°C).

What Would I See if I Went to Saturn?

After traveling through the darkness of outer space, you would see Saturn glowing golden as you approached. The mystery of Saturn's golden glow was not solved until the National Aeronautics and Space Administration (NASA) sent **space probes** to the ringed **planet.**

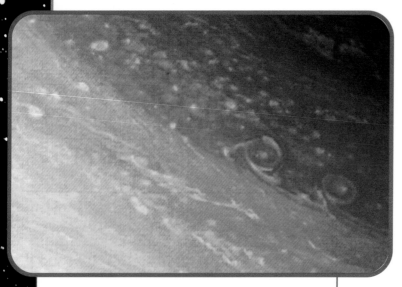

The bands you see in pictures of Saturn are bands of clouds moving rapidly around the planet. Each band moves at a slightly different speed.

Thick layers of clouds cover Saturn. NASA's probes provided information about the types of gases in the **atmosphere** of Saturn that give these clouds their color. Light rays from the **Sun** strike the clouds and make them shine brightly.

A light show

The combination of **solar wind** and Saturn's magnetic field causes Saturn to have **auroras** at its poles. Stray particles from the Sun are pulled in by the magnetic field and crash together, giving off energy in the form of light. This makes the sky fill with blues, reds, and greens in wavy patterns. An aurora on Saturn is like the northern lights on Earth, only much brighter.

A bumpy ride

Flying through the rings would be a bumpy ride because of all of the ice crystals that would bang into your spaceship. Saturn also has a very strong magnetic field around it and high levels of radiation. The magnetic field traps charged particles from the Sun, which creates the radiation.

Floating through the atmosphere

Once you get through the magnetic field, you would enter the atmosphere. Most of Saturn's atmosphere is made of hydrogen gas. Saturn's atmosphere has more hydrogen than any planet. Some of the hydrogen is combined with other chemicals. The rest of the atmosphere is mostly helium gas. Helium is used here on Earth to make balloons float in the air.

Close-up photographs of the rings like this one help scientists to study them more easily.

Saturn's cloud layers

The **atmosphere** of Saturn has three thick layers of clouds. When you look at Saturn through a **telescope** or at a picture from a **space probe,** the "surface" that you see is really the cloud layers that cover Saturn. The outer cloud layers are about 250 miles (400 kilometers) deep.

Each of Saturn's three cloud layers is different. The top cloud layer is made of ammonia crystals. Frozen ammonia crystals look like tiny pieces of hail. They float in the clouds high up in the atmosphere of Saturn.

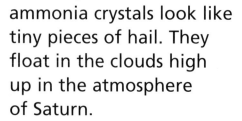

Ammonia gas freezes into crystals because the temperatures in this layer are much colder than those in the cloud layers deeper inside Saturn. The top cloud layer looks pale and creamy.

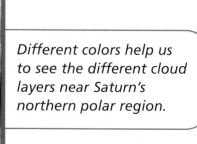

Different colors help us to see the different cloud layers near Saturn's northern polar region.

The middle cloud layer of Saturn is made of a different type of ammonia crystal mixed with hydrogen and **sulfur.** This layer is red and brown.

The bottom cloud layer is a hazy color of grayish blue. It is made of frozen water crystals and ammonia droplets. Earth's clouds have water droplets that we call rain.

Scientists do not know what the atmosphere is like below the bottom cloud layer. Future space probes may answer this question.

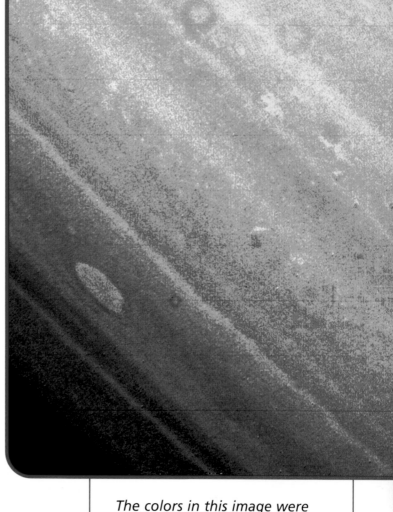

The colors in this image were adjusted to make Saturn's red spot easier to see.

No ground to stand on

Saturn does not have a surface. The atmosphere simply gets thicker and thicker until it is a liquid. Scientists do not think there is any water in this layer of Saturn.

Many, many moons

If you like looking at Earth's Moon, you could have a lot of fun on Saturn. As you fly through the **atmosphere** of Saturn, you would see at least eighteen **moons.** Thirteen of these moons were discovered during a **ring-plane crossing.** That is when the rings are flat across, which makes it easier to see what else is **orbiting** Saturn.

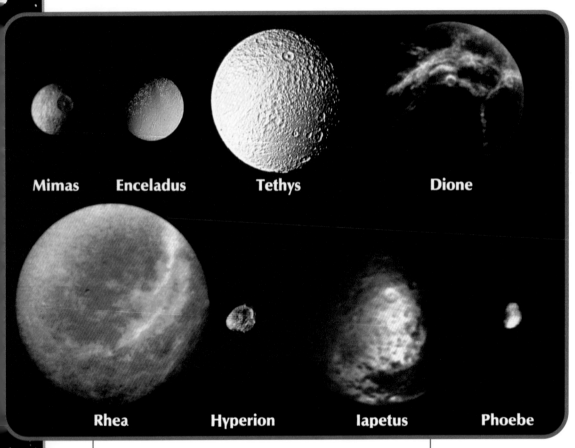

Mimas   Enceladus   Tethys   Dione

Rhea   Hyperion   Iapetus   Phoebe

These are eight of Saturn's many moons.

New moons are being discovered all the time. All seem to be made mostly of rock and ice. Four more were found during the ring-plane crossing in 1995. Of the five moons discovered at other times, one was first discovered in 1898. The other four were seen in images from the *Voyager* **space probes** in 1980 and 1981. Scientists are not sure of the total number of moons Saturn might have. There may be more than 30.

Titan, the orange moon

Titan is the largest of Saturn's moons and the second largest moon in the **solar system.** It is even bigger than the **planets** Mercury and Pluto. Titan looks like a smooth, orange ball. It was the first of Saturn's moons that scientists discovered. Titan is the only moon in the solar system that has an atmosphere. The small amount of methane gas in its atmosphere makes the moon look orange. This methane also makes the clouds on Titan. Most of Titan's atmosphere is made up of **nitrogen** gas, just like in Earth's atmosphere.

No one has seen Titan's surface. Information from the *Voyager* missions showed that the surface might be covered with lakes of liquid ethane—a thick, oily chemical found in gasoline. Below this may be layers of frozen methane and ammonia. Titan's surface temperature is about −290°F (−180°C). Titan is about 3,000 miles (5,000 kilometers) wide.

Titan is about 750,000 miles (1.2 million kilometers) away from Saturn.

Enceladus, the brightest moon

Enceladus is completely covered by frozen ice. This makes it the brightest **moon** in our **solar system.** All the sunlight that reaches this moon is reflected, just like a mirror reflects all of the light that strikes its surface. Enceladus is much smaller than Earth's Moon.

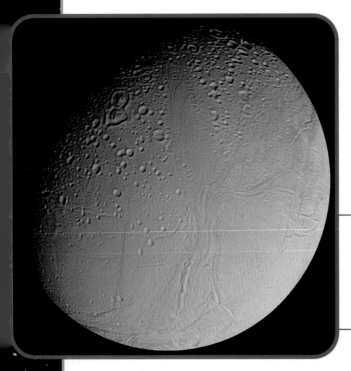

Enceladus is only 310 miles (500 kilometers) wide. It is about 110,600 miles (178,000 kilometers) away from Saturn.

Mimas

Mimas, another of Saturn's moons, is made up almost entirely of frozen water and is much smaller than Earth's Moon. Long ago a very large object crashed into the surface of Mimas. Scientists think that if the object had been any bigger, it might have broken Mimas into little pieces.

If packed tightly, more than 650 moons the size of Mimas could fit inside Earth's moon.

Mimas did not break up, but it has the largest **crater** for an object of its size in the entire solar system. The crater is about 80 miles (130 kilometers) across and 6 miles (10 kilometers) deep. If there were a highway running through the crater, it would take you about one and a half hours to drive from one end to the other.

In this photo of Saturn, the moon Tethys is above the moon Dione. The shadow of Tethys is near the bottom of the image just below the rings.

Does Saturn have any other moons?

Saturn also has some moons that scientists call **shepherd moons.** These moons **orbit** within or come very close to Saturn's rings. Any stray ring materials that might otherwise pull away are kept in orbit by these moons. They act like shepherds bringing stray sheep back to the flock. There may be many more shepherd moons that scientists have yet to discover.

What Is Inside Saturn?

Below the cloud layers of Saturn is a layer of hydrogen gas. Below that is a very deep sea of liquid hydrogen mixed with helium. There is no clear border between the gas in the **atmosphere** and the sea of liquid hydrogen. The two layers of the planet sort of blend together.

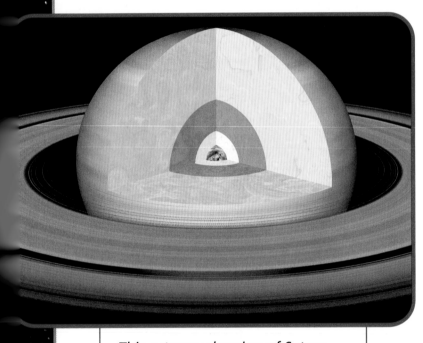

This cutaway drawing of Saturn shows where its different layers start. The layers blend together more than this artwork can show.

At the bottom of the liquid layer, the hydrogen is weighed down by all the hydrogen and helium above. The weight makes the hydrogen take on a different form. It acts like a metal that has been melted into a liquid. Scientists call this metallic hydrogen.

Only Saturn's **core,** at the center of the **planet,** is solid. Scientists do not know for sure what Saturn's core is made of, but they think it is rock and ice. Saturn's core is about the same size as Earth. The core temperature is about 9,000°F (5,000°C). That is nearly as hot as the surface of the **Sun!** The icy core can only exist at such high temperatures because the pressure is so strong.

Could I Ever Go to Saturn?

Do you have a lot of time and money?

It takes over three years to get to Saturn. It would be very expensive to build a spacecraft large enough to hold astronauts and enough food and equipment for such a long journey. And that is just to get there. You would still have to get back to Earth. Communicating with the mission control center on Earth would also be difficult. It takes more than an hour for a radio signal to travel between Earth and Saturn, even at the speed of light. It there was an emergency and you needed help, the help might arrive too late. Going to Saturn would be difficult and dangerous.

You can look at the pictures, instead

On October 1, 1958, the United States created an organization to study space. They called it the National Aeronautics and Space Administration (NASA). Over time, NASA has become one of the world's leading groups for studying outer space.

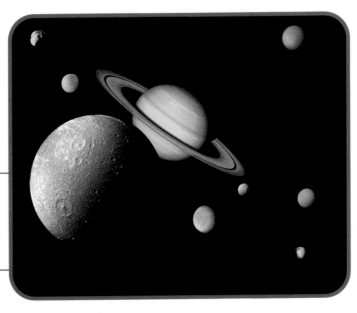

*This collection of images shows Saturn and eight of its **moons.***

The *Pioneer* mission to Saturn

In April 1973, NASA sent the *Pioneer 11* **space probe** to study Jupiter and Saturn. In September 1979, *Pioneer 11* flew past Saturn from 13,000 miles (20,921 kilometers) away. It took the first close-up pictures of Saturn. They discovered two new **moons** and another ring, and they found that the moon Titan is too cold to support life.

This is an artist's idea of what it looked like when Pioneer 11 was reaching Saturn.

The *Voyager* missions

In 1977, NASA sent two space probes, *Voyager 1* and *Voyager 2,* to study Saturn, Jupiter, Uranus, and Neptune. *Voyager 1* first arrived near Saturn in November 1980. It sent back photos of Saturn's rings. The photos showed that dark, shadowy fingers pointing outward sometimes form in Saturn's rings. These are called "spokes." Scientists now believe that these spokes are made of clouds of tiny particles that float above the rings. They are shaped by the powerful magnetic field of Saturn.

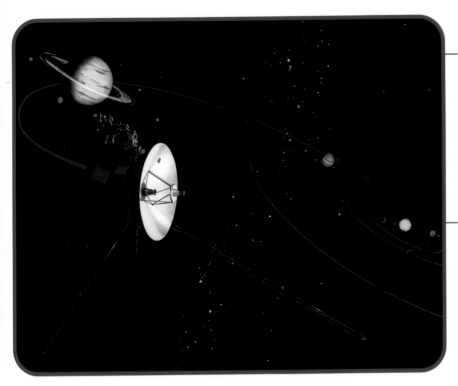

An artist illustrated this vision of what the Voyager mission looked like in outer space.

Where are the *Voyagers* now?

In 1991 *Voyager 1's* Saturn mission was complete. It continued on in outer space. Eleven years later, when it was 3.7 billion miles (6 billion kilometers) from the **Sun,** it sent back a picture of all of the **planets** in the **solar system.** Scientists hope that *Voyager 1* will be able to continue traveling through space in working order through the year 2040. It should continue working until at least 2015.

After visiting Saturn, *Voyager 2* continued on to Uranus and Neptune. More than twenty years after it was launched, *Voyager 2* is still flying through space. Scientists hope that *Voyager 2* will be able to continue working through the year 2034.

The *Cassini* mission

In October 1997, NASA launched one of the largest, heaviest **space probes** ever. The *Cassini* mission is expected to last over ten years. The probe will visit Saturn and its largest **moon,** Titan. *Cassini* should reach Saturn in 2004. The Italian Space Agency (ASI) and the European Space Agency (ESA) are two of the many groups helping NASA with the project.

This is an artist's impression of the Cassini orbiter as the Huygens probe separated from it to enter the **atmosphere** *of Saturn.*

The *Cassini* spacecraft has an **orbiter** that will study the **planet** from above the surface for about four years. During that time, it will release a small spacecraft called the *Huygens* probe.

The *Huygens* probe will travel to Saturn's biggest moon, Titan. Its parachutes and heat shield will help it to land safely on the moon. The probe is expected to take more than 1,000 pictures of Titan. It will send these pictures to the orbiter. The orbiter will then send the pictures back to Earth.

When will *Cassini* get to Saturn?

The *Cassini* mission will take about seven years to reach Saturn. If it flew straight from Earth to Saturn, it would take much less time. But a longer distance will end up saving rocket fuel. *Cassini* will first fly in **orbits** around Venus and Earth. The **gravity** from each of these planets works like a slingshot to give the space probe a big boost in speed. Then it will fly past Jupiter. Jupiter's strong gravity will "whip" the space probe toward its final target, Saturn.

What else do we know about the *Cassini* mission?

- *Cassini* will travel about 2 billion miles (3.2 billion kilometers) just to reach Saturn. This is very far. To travel the same distance, the *Cassini* would have to fly to Earth's Moon and back more than 4,219 times!

- *Cassini* will travel at very fast speeds. At one point, it will travel so fast it would be like flying from the west coast to the east coast of the United States in about five minutes!

- On its way to Saturn, *Cassini* is supposed to "whip" around Venus twice and around Earth once to use each planet's gravity to build up speed. These orbits will save the ship more than 75 tons (68,040 kilograms) of rocket fuel.

Fact File

	SATURN	EARTH
Average distance from the Sun	887 million miles (1,427 million kilometers)	93 million miles (150 million kilometers)
Revolution around the Sun	29.5 Earth years	1 Earth year (365 days)
Average speed of orbit	6.0 miles/second (9.7 kilometers/second)	18.6 miles/second (30 kilometers/second)
Diameter at equator	74,898 miles (120,536 kilometers)	7,926 miles (12,756 kilometers)
Time for one rotation	10 hours, 39 minutes	24 hours
Atmosphere	hydrogen, helium	oxygen, nitrogen
Moons	at least 30	1
Temperature range	−312°F (−191°C) to −92°F (−69°C)	−92°F (−69°C) to 136°F (58°C)

This image shows a lot more detail of the rings of Saturn than many other images of the planet. The shadow of the rings can be seen on the surface of the planet.

A trip to Saturn from Earth

- When Saturn and Earth come closest to each other in their **orbits,** they are 793 million miles (1.28 billion kilometers) apart.

- Traveling by car at 70 miles (113 kilometers) per hour, the trip would take at least 1,292 years.

- Traveling by rocket at 7 miles (11 kilometers) per second, the trip would take at least 3 years and 7 months.

More interesting facts:

- Suppose you traveled in a **space probe** from Saturn's inside ring to its outside ring. You would travel over 170,000 miles (273,530 kilometers) during your trip. To travel this distance on Earth, you would have to fly in a plane almost seven times around Earth.

- Saturn has more **moons** than any other **planet** in our **solar system.** Stray **asteroids** continue to get caught in Saturn's **gravity,** becoming new moons.

- Saturn has one moon, called Phoebe, that spins in the opposite direction of all the other moons of the planet.

Cassini's Gap is in the lower righthand corner of this image. Color filters were used to make the rings brighter and easier to see in this image.

Glossary

asteroid   large piece of floating rock left over from when the planets formed

astronomer   person who studies objects in outer space

atmosphere   all of the gases that surround an object in outer space

aurora   colorful display caused by charged particles in an atmosphere

axis   imaginary line through the middle of an object in space, around which it spins as it rotates

comet   ball of ice and rock that orbits around the Sun

core   center of a planet

crater   bowl-shaped hole in the ground that is made by a meteorite or a burst of lava

day   time it takes for a planet to spin around its axis one time

density   amount of stuff something is made of compared to how much space it takes up

equator   imaginary line around the middle of a planet

gravity   invisible force that pulls objects toward the center of another object in outer space

meteorite   piece of rock or dust that lands on the surface of a planet or a moon from space

moon   object that floats in an orbit around a planet

nitrogen   gas found in the atmosphere of Earth and some of the other planets in our solar system

orbit   curved path of one object in space moving around another object

orbiter   spaceship that flies in orbit around a planet

planet   large object in space that orbits a central star, has an atmosphere, and does not produce its own light

revolution   time it takes for a planet to travel one time around the Sun (also known as a year)

revolve   to travel one time around the Sun; or, for a moon to travel one time around a planet

ringlet   single ring of orbiting dust or ice that combines with other ringlets to form a ring around an object in outer space

ring-plane crossing   when all the rings of a planet are lined up to be flat across from a person's point of view

shepherd moons   moons in orbit around Saturn's rings that keep material in the rings from breaking out of orbit

solar system   group of objects in outer space that all float in orbits around a central star

solar wind   material continually coming off of the Sun's surface and traveling through space

space probe   ship that carries computers and other instruments to study objects in outer space

star   large ball of gas in outer space; produces its own light by burning gases

sulfur   yellow-colored, powdery material; found on many planets in gas form

Sun   central star in our solar system

telescope   instrument used by astronomers to study objects in outer space

year   time it takes for a planet to orbit the Sun one time

More Books to Read

Brimner, Larry Dane. *Saturn.* Danbury, Conn.: Children's Press, 1999.

Kerrod, Robin. *Saturn.* Minneapolis, Minn.: Lerner Publications, 2000.

Landau, Elaine. *Saturn.* Danbury, Conn.: Franklin Watts, 1996.

Index

atmosphere   11, 12, 13, 14, 15, 16, 17
auroras   14
axis   10

Cassini, Giovanni   7
Cassini space probe   26, 26, 27
Cassini's Gap   7
Chapelain, Jean   8
cloud layers   16–17
clouds   11, 14
core   13, 22

days   6
density   9
Dione (moon)   18, 21

Enceladus (moon)   18, 20
European Space Agency (ESA)   26

Galilei, Galileo   5, 9
gravity   4
Great White Spot   12

helium gas   15, 22
Huygens, Christiaan   5, 9, 10
Huygens space probe   26–27
hydrogen gas   15, 22
Hyperion (moon)   18

Iapetus (moon)   18
Italian Space Agency (ASI)   26

magnetic field   14, 15, 24
Maxwell, James Clerk   8
metallic hydrogen   22
Mimas (moon)   18, 20–21
moons   4, 10, 18–21, 23, 24, 26

name   5
National Aeronautics and Space Administration (NASA)   14, 23

orbit   4, 6, 8

Phoebe (moon)   18
Pioneer 11 space probe   24

radiation   15
revolution   6
Rhea (moon)   18
rings   4, 7, 8, 9, 10, 13, 15, 21, 24

Saturn   4, 7, 9, 10, 11, 13, 21, 23, 24
Saturnus (Roman god)   5
shepherd moons   21
size   4
solar system   4, 5, 6
space probes   11, 19, 24, 25, 26–27
spokes   24

storms   12, 13
Sun   4
surface   17

temperature   11, 13
Tethys (moon)   18, 21
Titan (moon)   19, 24, 26

Voyager space probes   19, 24, 25

weather   11–13
winds   11, 12

years   6